THE ADVENTURES OF
DERBY CALIFORNIA
Derby Learns to Surf

written by   written by   illustrated by

Kentucky Gallahue   Glenn G. Millar   Ashley Lanni

Acknowledgements

Derby and I have many people to thank for helping us turn our dream of writing a children's book into reality. To all of our amazing fans who have followed us on our crazy adventures, you guys are the best! Thank you so much for the love and support. To my friends and family, thank you for the encouragement to follow my dreams and hang out with my dog every day. Without your love and support we would not be able to do what we do, putting smiles on everyone's faces. Finally to Kenia, my love and my everything. Thank you for being the brains behind Derby California and for keeping Derby and I alive. Everyone knows being an adult is hard for me and running a business is even harder. None of this would be possible without you.

~Kentucky

As I was writing this book, I imagined reading it to 3 very special children, Mckenzie, Aiden and Grace (and in this writer's non-biased opinion, the smartest, most charming and best looking children on the planet.) With every sentence I thought, "Would they like it?" This book is dedicated to you. I love you so much. I would like to thank Amanda, who is not only their Mother, but truly the best Mother I have ever known. Your selfless love, your encouragement, and your dedication to your children is entwined in this book in the interactions between Kentucky and Derby. Finally, to Alexandra: I have a lot of dreams. You have always supported all of them no matter how insane. The only reason I wrote this book was because when one day I asked you, "Could I write a children's book?" you didn't hesitate in your answer, "Of course you can. It will be great." Without you, your support and your encouragement, this book and many of my dreams would not be possible. I love you.

~Glenn

Thank you Josh for the encouragement, and to Sandor and Liko for all the company at the drawing desk during the late nights. I really do have the best life.

~Ashley

Thank you to Ben Higginbotham for video contributions, Charmaine Gray, Dale Portre, and Brett Frager for picture contributions, and Ashley Ryan Larrabee for logo creation.

Dale Portre

ISBN 978-0-578-28571-9

First Edition June 2022

This book used Playtime with Hot Toddies, Duality and Cutie Patootie fonts.

All illustrations were made with pencil and digital.

Printed in China

Look for **QR** codes throughout the book to see real videos of Kentucky and **Derby**!

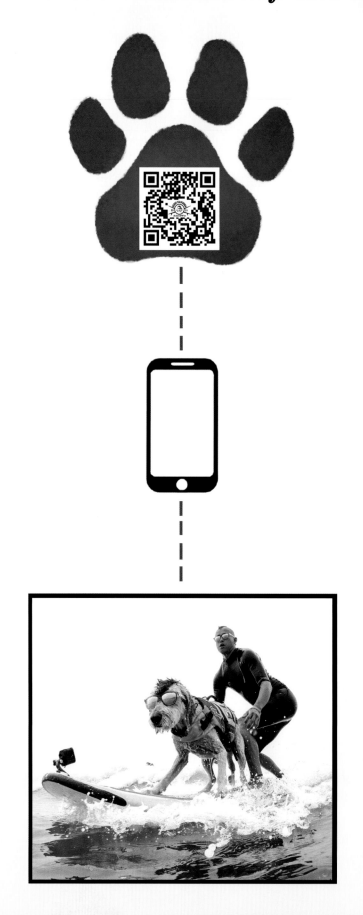

Hey Y'all!

Today is my first surf contest. I am so excited! My name is Derby. I'm a Goldendoodle, and I love adventure. But it wasn't always like that. Not very long ago I was just a scared little puppy. Then I met the man with the blue mohawk. And that's where my story begins...

"LOOK AT THAT PUPPY!

I LOVE HIM!"

That's the first thing I heard the man with the blue mohawk say. He was talking about me! I was so excited! Could he be my new best friend?

"Hey, little buddy. My name is Kentucky," said the man with the blue mohawk. "Let's call you Derby. Do you want to be my friend and come home with me?"

I think the man with the blue mohawk could tell I was feeling a little scared.

"Don't worry, Derby. I promise I'll take great care of you and take you on lots of fun adventures." That's when he gave me a big hug.

We got into his blue pickup truck and left for the big city. As we drove, the roads got bigger. There were so many cars, trucks, and buses all around us.

I did not like all of the noises. I wanted to go back home.

"It's ok," said the man with the blue mohawk.
"Loud noises can be very scary. I promise to
always protect you and be there for you." Then
he gave me a big hug. I felt so much better.

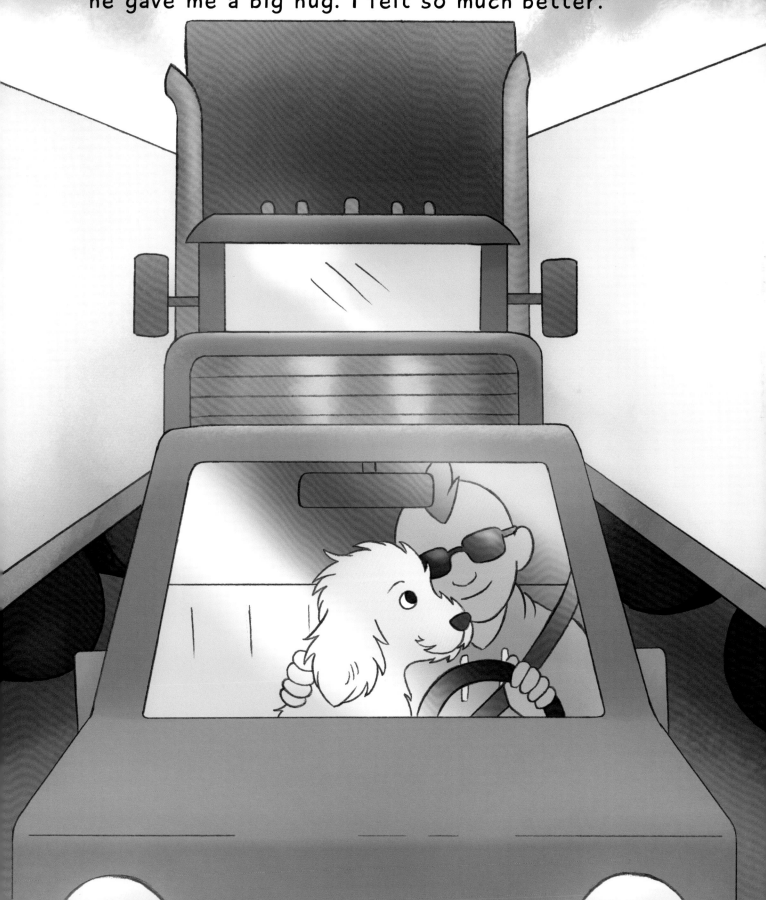

The next few months were really exciting. The man with the blue mohawk took me on walks every day.

We met so many people, but none of them had cool blue hair like my new best friend.

I loved all the different dogs I got to meet.

Big dogs!

Short dogs!

Fluffy dogs!

Shaggy dogs!

BARK BARK

Yappie dogs!

Pretty dogs wearing clothes!

The best part was hanging out with the man with the blue mohawk. Every day was a different adventure.

Camping

Canoeing

Swimming

Baseball games

Eating at restaurants

Car trips

Scooter rides

Bike rides

We had so much fun together!

Not long after that, the man with the blue mohawk started to teach me tricks. He taught me to sit, to shake, and to roll over. Those were easy tricks. I was proud that I learned them so fast and was ready for the fun ones, like catching a Frisbee!

I love playing catch!

The man with the blue mohawk also taught me to pick up things like the TV remote control. He thinks I'm doing him a favor, but when he isn't looking, I like to change the channel to my favorite cartoons.

One day, while the man with the blue mohawk was getting his hair done, I thought, "I want a blue mohawk too!"

So I picked up the bottle of blue dye and brought it to him.

"Derby, you know what? We should give you a blue mohawk too!" I let him think it was his idea.

"Look at our new haircuts, Derby. We look like twins."

"Together we can do anything!"

"It's time for a new adventure," the man with the blue mohawk said to me one day. "We're moving to California!"

"Oh boy!" I thought. "Swimmin' pools and movie stars!"

So we loaded up the blue pickup truck and said goodbye.

It was a long trip to California. We drove for many days.

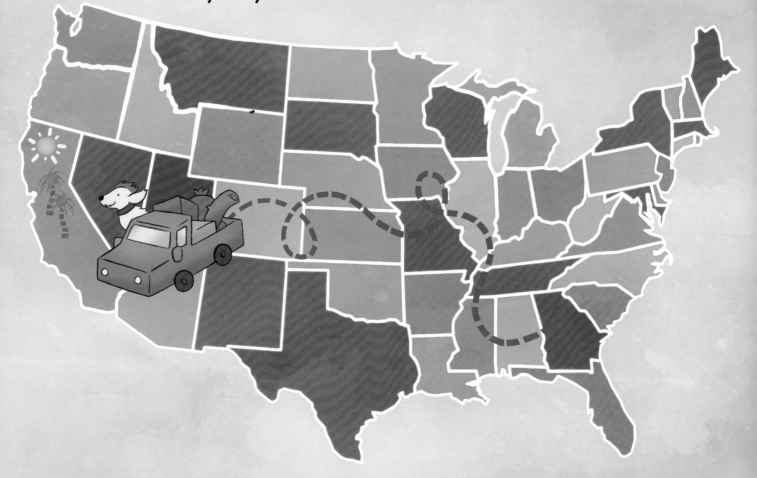

"Hey Buddy. Wake up. We're here!"

I jumped out of the blue truck and felt warm sand under my paws. Seeing the ocean for the first time was amazing.

There was water as far as I could see. Waves were crashing in front of us. There were even seagulls to chase. I knew I was going to like it here.

We settled into our new home. A few weeks later, the man said, "Want to watch me learn to surf tomorrow?"

"I'd love to!" I thought.

"What's surfing?"

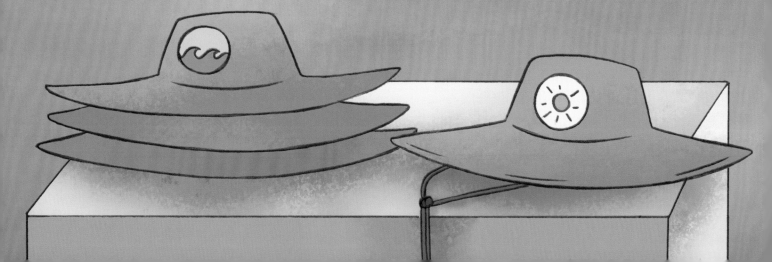

The man with the blue mohawk went into the ocean with his new surfboard. Every time a wave came in, the surfers would stand up on their boards and ride the wave. It looked pretty easy to me.

The man with the blue mohawk didn't make it look very easy though. Every time he stood up, he ended up falling off his surfboard. He was having fun, but he seemed to spend more time in the ocean than surfing.

I ran into the surf, just in case he needed to be rescued. When I got to him, he asked, "Derby, do you want to try this?" I jumped on the board and wagged my tail.

The first wave came in and the man gave me a push. Wheeee! I was flying! It was so much fun! I rode that wave all the way to the beach. Other surfers were looking at me. I don't think they had ever seen a surfing dog before. I bet they wish they had four paws.

That was the best day ever! We started surfing all the time. Sometimes I surfed itty-bitty waves.

Sometimes they were ginormous.

Sometimes I
surfed alone.

Sometimes
with the man with
the blue mohawk.

I even learned to surf backwards.

I had just surfed a great wave when I saw someone passing out flyers. I took one to the man with the blue mohawk.

DOG SURFING COMPETITION
For dogs and their 2-legged friends

He looked at it and grinned. "A surf competition...FOR DOGS??? What an awesome idea! What do you think, Derby? Should I sign us up?"

I was wagging my tail furiously because I wanted to try it. But part of me was scared. What if I didn't do well?

The day of the surf competition I was feeling pretty nervous. I didn't want to tell the man with the blue mohawk, because he was so excited and I didn't want to hurt his feelings.

"What's wrong, Derby?" said the man.
"Are you feeling OK?"
   I was so glad he asked! He really cared
about my feelings. What if I made a fool of
myself in front of the other dogs?

"Guess what, Derby? I have a present for you!"

That was the day I got my first pair of sunglasses. They felt magical, and I wasn't nervous anymore. I was confident, just like the man with the blue mohawk.

"Surfing is all about having a good time," said the man. "It doesn't matter if you win or lose today. You can even wipe out on every wave. No one is going to laugh at you. Surfing is just hanging out with your friends, enjoying the sun, and playing in the water."

I felt so much better. I didn't have to impress anyone. I was just going to have fun with my best friend Kentucky.

So that's exactly what I did. I had so much fun competing and surfing with my new four-legged friends.

That's my story. I went from being a scared little puppy, to meeting my best friend Kentucky, to becoming Derby California, the surfing dog.

Of course, there have been many other fun and exciting adventures since then. I can't wait to tell you all about them next time!

THE END

Told you it was a mostly true story...

Brett Frager

Charmaine Gray

Dale Portre